Pieces of Me

Siera Shroyer

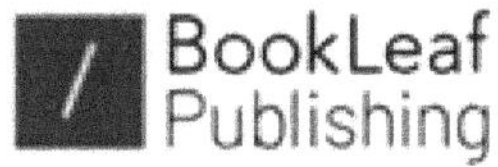

Presentation by *BookLeaf Publishing*

Web: www.bookleafpub.com

E-mail: info@bookleafpub.com

ISBN: 9789357211079

First edition 2022

DEDICATION

To anybody that needs to know what makes me "Me"......

To my mother, for pushing me to do what I dream, and not settle for anything less. To my father, for showing me that I am me, and that is what I am best at being....and that is priceless.

To my daughter, always convincing me to be brave, and to break out of my shell.... and to everyone else I love, because you all have helped me become more!!!!

~Thank you~

PREFACE

"As a daughter, sister, mother, friend, poet, author, teacher, student, lover, sinner, failure, dreamer, and a fresh new successor, I am "making it" by giving you these gems of mine, to see me for me. From a small-town girl, with a huge heart, an endless imagination, a crazy mind, and a kind soul, I now offer one of the most intimate gifts i have to offer--- I give to you: my words."

~Always~

Be impeccable with your word-
The word is a force; It's your tool of magic that enables you to "create" your life, and your reality. Misuse of your word, therefore, can destroy your life, make reality into hell. What you dream, feel, believe, experience, and intend all manifest through your WORD.

Don't take anything personally-
Personal importance is the maximum expression of selfishness, because we assume that everything is all about 'ME'. Nothing others do is because of you, it is because of them, their own issues, purposes, motives and influences.

Don't make assumptions-
The problem with assumptions is that we tend to believe them to be the truth. We believe them to be real, so we take it personally, which creates blame and doubt, which leads to total misunderstanding... all over literally nothing. Always ask any and everything it takes to be as clear as possible about everything. Don't be afraid to know all you can about anything, so chaos can't make us misinterpret or misunderstand each other.

Always do your best-
No more, no less; Your best will vary ongoingly
and will change over time, which is all okay. If
you always do your best, in that moment, there's
no way to doubt or judge yourself. As life goes
on, you learn that you are here to "LIVE", to be
happy, to love, not to sacrifice your joy or your
life. In doing your best, you take action because
you love it, not because you expect rewards that
don't come, creating regrets.
Action is about living life to the fullest. Inaction
is denying life. Let the past go, live in the now to
be fully "ALIVE"!

ALWAYS IMAGINE.

~The Path of Life~

The path has come full circle once more ...
The final gathering has now begun.
Have we learned how to do it right this time...?
Have we the strength to stand again as one?
Have we faith in what's right and good?
Have we knowledge enough to know what must
be done?
With the end comes a new beginning ...
of what we are truly meant to be.
It's really, so very simple,
You see- We've always had the key.
It's the one thing that can't be bought or stolen,
It can only be given, and it is always free.
It is the unconditional love that we share ...
It's been right here, all along, inside you and me!

~What Is~

Death is ...
gunshots echoing through the night
bloodstains on the street
friends gathered at the grave
an empty hole in your heart
a brother who never came home.

Knowledge is ...
staying in school
doing homework
learning from your elders
having power
understanding.

Gentle is ...
a soft spring breeze
petals on a rose
a newborn baby
wings of a butterfly
a hug from the one you love.

Doubt is ...
broken promises
lies
distrust

a miscommunication
a person's past reputation.

5

Caring is ...
a helping hand
doing a favor
a shoulder to cry on
being understanding
a hand to hold.

~Mixed Emotions~

Weary is my heart and soul, for too many times
they've been broken ...
People pretending to care, deceiving me, while
lies are spoken.
Only thinking of themselves, they plant a seed
and summon the rain,
Then watch it tear worlds into pieces, without
feeling a single ounce of pain.
There's much too much pain in our lives today.
There's no need for bringing on the rain!
All my intentions are good, all my love is true,
Everything I am, I give and share with you.
Somewhere, somehow, I lost the you I knew.
All I ever tried to do was be good to you, and
see things through ...
but I don't know how to get us through this
Don't know what to do about it!
Wish that I could make everything better.
I believed that we would be together forever ...
Now I think that I should have known better
than to think that you were ever my forever ...
As time goes on, things don't change,
Nothing seems to be right.
It breaks my heart, and hurts my soul
To even know that we now fight.

It breaks my heart, and it makes me cry!
To think that we could one day say goodbye...

~Life Is...~

Life is ...
Watching the small things grow into bigger ones,
Taking time to listen to another story from a
stranger,
Driving too fast, sometimes,
Screaming so loud that your throat is raw, and
your
voice is almost gone at a concert,
Playing card games to entertain yourself and
your siblings,
Leaving the house, when you wish you could
just stay home,
Hearing the sounds of an old creaky rocking
chair,
Learning that your dad will never come home,
Wondering how it feels to fall in love with
someone,
Fearing what their answer will be,
if they hate you, or if they love you back,
Counting the stars in the midnight sky,
And, wondering what they feel,
Talking with your mom one day,
and the next day she's gone,

Walking down the shoreline and gathering
seashells,
Playing music with your friends all night long,
until the sun comes up again.
Keeping your eyes open whenever you get
kissed,
Helping people appreciate each day,
seeing beauty in all of the world's amiss,
Believing in love, speaking the truth,
While embracing life's chaotic symphony.

~Of Them...~

Few will listen...
Of the few who listen, fewer still will
understand.
Understanding does not mean that they believe.
Of the handful who do believe,
Most may know not what to do.
Of those who even know,
How many will actually DO?
As for the rare ones, the ones who have done it...
They need not live with this anymore...

Where no light can shine,
no shadow can pass.
Delicious, must look heaven,
to the hungry in hell...
to the starving soul,
every bitter thing tastes sweet,
until eternity
the "man" in orange
is damned to writhe within the "Pitts"
of Westwood's frozen, lamplit streets
waiting... for souls to meet...

Eternally scarred by the lessons learned,
Memories remain within my mind,

They will reside here, inside my heart,
Until the end of time.
Innocence lost to war, never to return,
It won't ever let you be,
Never free! Never me!
If I believe in you,
Will you believe in me?
I am the shore, and you are the sea.
What I've felt, What I've known,
Burn the pages, crush the stone.
This is the time... it is the moment!
Become what fate has come to show me.
Home
Free to be free, with me,
living the life , it is destined to be,
That what we have last beyond infinity...
Just believe and it shall be!

~Beautiful Butterflies~

You can fly if you want to,
Go as high as you want to,
All you have to do is believe in you,
That's all you've got to do.
You can cry if you want to,
Do whatever you need.
Let your soul shine through,
you know, you have to believe.
You can dream if you want to,
just let all your thoughts run free.
You'll be whatever you want to,
That will be right next to me!
The only thing that tears it apart
are the ones who should be closest to my heart.
They push it all away,
Therefore, put it all on hold one more day.
Boy, oh, boy!
Does that get old fast?
I can't believe it had to be this way,
But I need this time to last-
It's like going back into your past,
As your future unfolds before you...
Remember that nothing lasts forever,
Even though, it's sad but true.
But, in my heart, nothing else matters

than for this all to be real.
You can do anything you want to,
All it takes is a dream, some hope, and a little
blind faith,
To know that you're loved, so I am too,
And cared for by one another,
Mother, daughter, son, or any other.
Let your true colors of light
Shine through you, so true!
Let us into your life, and your mind.
You've finally come back into view ...
Always remember these words I tell you now,
Because this is how you will understand:

You can fly if you want to,
  You just have to believe!
Faith, Trust, and Love
Let them take the lead;
So always keep a dream in your heart-
  That's how you keep from falling apart.
Keep everything under control-
  because, now opens the magic hole,
Into a world of chaos, and treasures, untold...
  This is what our future holds ...

Don't ever let it beat you.
You're better than that.

~Tips For the Road~

Strike a match, light the sky, hold on tight.
 The day suddenly slipped away, the world,
destroyed, during that very night.
 The fierce burn of hatred, the horrid flames of
fear,
 They're always creeping, nearer and nearer.
 Barely escaping from the pain, I turn ...

 The clouds above hide a spectacular paradise.
 That's where my soul shall rest- after I finish
this test.
 The power of love, warmth, and security,
 The brilliant shine of joy, casted by the
shimmering stars.
 Through the smoke and ashes
 Rises the goodness that was hidden, so far
away,
 As it's strength and purity guides us on our way
It'll begin a new day.
 A new place to explore, the right way.
 A new world to share,
 A new game to play ...

The fire shall cleanse, and only the phoenix

Can rise out of the ashes again, and again.
It's spirit remains true,
After all it goes through.
Same for us,
The things we've been put through.
Our souls are exceptional,
Like each star that touches the sky.
It's possible that you may
never look up at those stars again.
Just because a match was lighted
The fire in the sky ignited.
The fire spread throughout the sky,
And people began to scream and cry.
Their fears only made matters worse,
Giving the evil what they thirst.
The only way to win is to learn
How to give, and how to care;
How to love, and how to share;
Not fear, but trust,
Not hate, but love,
We could create a union and rise above
All of the violence, pain, and disruption
The confusion of life,
My own destruction.

Out of the ashes and
Back on my feet again,
I wonder," Where will this road end?'
Some tips for the road,

Just incase you need some
Guidelines or instructions:
*Be wise, and keep your head about you at all
times.
*Be bold, and stand your ground
*Be considerate, and caring, it's the only way to
be.
*Stick together.
*The doing will be done without doing.
*Gain patience and knowledge.
*Don't sit and worry, it makes things worse.

~Concept~

We, the unwilling,

  Lead by the unqualified,

    have been doing the unbelievable,
     so long, with so little;

  We now will attempt the impossible

    with nothing.....

  This is just a little thought/theory of my many
thoughts and - hey!- it's just a simple concept!

~Moments~

Smile, laugh, enjoy these moments! They cannot
stay....
Please lean on me, for I am your rock.
I am your strength when you are not strong.
I am the light in the darkest of night.
I am the beat, the beat beneath your feet;
heartbeat of life, filling your life with sound.
Music, movement, rhythm, melody; memory,
harmony, symphony,
destiny, eternity, forever moving gracefully
through time.
Existing only within our kind, within our minds;
The spell that binds;
Release your souls;
Complete freedom!
Thankful for what makes us whole;
Less control now; Believe, let go, be only you
not for the world, because this life is the only
one we have to learn from.
Live life to it's fullest, and learn something new
every day...
Because before we know it, it will come to the
end.
Love -- it makes it all worth it!

Nothing else matters. I wouldn't have it any
other way.

19

~Blank~

The cold light of day fills this room,
Only the pillow knows how I feel.
Curtains of blue, and sheets of white keep me
company
 through this long and lonely fight.
Four walls face me at all times,
and the posters watch my every move.
Madness seeps into my head,
the ceiling hangs there lifelessly,
 limp, and dead.... Blank.
The black light covers this room,
the darkness blinds me for a bittersweet
moment.
The truth is a forgotten language
that swims in endless pools of pure rage.
The air grows stale enough to breathe,
as the sadness brings out a strange joy.
Clouds roll away, leaving me alone once again;
Their shadows stain my walls;
The mirror reminds me of time long ago,
I had almost remembered the feeling of love.
I will survive, even though the life I pretend to
live doesn't seem to be worth the trouble. I feel
the storm slipping away again... I go blank.

~Love Is A Friendship~

Love is good;
Love is strong.
It goes through a friendship
all the year long.

That is why
it is so easy to say
"I do love you
in every way".

Love is for sisters,
Love is for friends,
Love is for people like me and you,
that hope it never ends

Since the moment we met,
so many years ago...
I knew our friendship
would do nothing but grow.

~Days Go By~

There is so much to learn from this life on earth!
Experiences affect us, from the moment of birth.
Impressions, connections, quarrels, conflicts,
Amusements, emotions, directions, intent
Exploring, composing, making each one of us
"unique",
all of these concepts make us complete.
Captured within our hearts, and souls,
a prize that's more precious than gold.
Never to be stolen, broken or sold.

With no bias of any kind, of any preface,
It makes no difference, the look of your face,
whether you're young, or old...short or tall,
shy, or bold, big or small,
poor or wealthy, dirty or clean.

It is the one thing keeping us all together,
the key to it all, makes life worth it, and all,
It's the beauty of LOVE.
It's the joy that binds us all together,
and holds on to our forever.

Love. Laugh. Live.

Enjoy life.

~A Friend~

A friend is someone you can trust, and who
would not turn away from you...
A friend will be there when you need someone,
and they will come to you when they need
help...
A friend will listen to you, even when they don't
understand or agree with your point of view...
A friend will NEVER try to change you, but
appreciates you for who you are...
A friend doesn't expect too much, nor give too
little.
A friend is someone you can share your dreams,
hopes, and fears with...
A friend is a person that you will suddenly smile
the moment you think of them, A friend accepts
your attitudes, ideas, and emotions, even when
their own are different than you...
A friend will hold your hand when you get
scared...
A friend will always tell you the truth, even
when it might hurt...
A friend will forgive you for the mistakes you've
made...
A friend will try not to disappoint you, and will
support you and share in your glory...

A friend shares responsibility when you have
doubts...
A friend always remembers the little things
you've done, the times you have shared, and the
talks you've had...
A friend will bend over backwards in order to
help you pick up the pieces...
When your world falls apart, a friend is one of
life's most wonderful parts
A friend is one of life's most beautiful gifts.

I am truly grateful to consider you to be my
friend.

~BeTrue~

25

You can say that you're sorry a million times
over,
Say, "I love you!", as much as you please.
Say whatever you want to, whenever you want
to.
Yet, if you are not going to prove to me
that these things that you say are true,
Then I'd rather you don't say anything at all.
Just let me be!! Leave me alone! And I will be
me, and you will be you.

~Music and People~

Knowing a person is like Music,
What attracts us to them
 is Thier Melody,
And as we Get to Know
 Who They are,
We begin to Learn Thier Lyrics...
A truth made to be let free.

~Choose Wisely~

In life,

you can choose to

Throw stones,

Stumble on them,

Climb over them,

Or build with them,

It's your choice.

You only get one life, so choose wisely.

~You See Me~

Encrypted upon these souls,
that seem destined to be together,
Forever, drenched, in the shadows of the
darkness within...
Where there lie the truths,
all of that will bring us to find our way home...
Together, lighting up the darkness
for only our eyes to see...
Living outside our minds, inside this life,
without a doubt, way out of control...
But... I know it now.
Please forgive my ignorance...
My eyes are wide open now...
I found just what I need...
I need to be me...
I have you to thank for helping me find,
within myself, the me I didn't see...
Insane as it might sound, I didn't realize
I'd been lost until I was found...
You found me.

****

Embracing the truth, entrusting the one
that holds every bit of my heart in their hands,

I tremble with fear, even though he is sincere,
the future becomes the present, then it's the past,
time moves way too fast!
I know things are scattered,
and look like a scheme,
Trust me, this could become
the real life version of reality of the dream.
I'll be waiting for the day to come
that people say just what they mean.
Until then, my world will be undone...
We both must breathe....
And always believe that life is, and it always
will be
ours to decide, and to live fearlessly... Free.

~A True Friend~

"What is a friend?", you ask
Well, I'll tell you...
It is a person with whom you can dare to be
yourself.
Your soul can be free, and go naked with him
The only thing he asks you to put on
is what you truly are, naked is your soul.
When you are with him, you do not have to be
on your guard,
You can speak freely, whatever you think,
So long as it is genuinely you.
He understands those contradictions in your
nature
that cause others to misjudge you.
With him, you breathe freely-
You can allow your little vanities, and envies,
and absurdities,
And by opening these insecurities up to him,
They then dissolve on the tides of his ocean of
loyalty.
He understands--You can weep with him, laugh
with him, pray with him---
through, and underneath it all, he sees, knows,
and loves you.

A Friend-I repeat- is one with whom you are
able to dare be yourself....
Any time, any place, no matter who is around...
He will be there, keeping you safe and sound.

~Someday~

Some day, when we have been together for a
very long time,
We'll turn out the lights, and slow dance on the
porch in our bath robes.
I'll write you love notes, in large print, and tape
them to the fridge.
You'll finish my stories, and I'll borrow your
glasses.
We'll wonder where the time went,
And each night, we'll roll to the middle of our
old bed,
into one another's arms, where we'll kiss and
touch,
holding each other's souls, as we drift of to
sleep,
and dream the secret dreams that only we get to
keep,
Dreams that only old lovers know....
and will keep for themselves, I know I do, so.

~Hold On!~

My life has been crazy, and it's no where near
over yet, so hold on tight, because:
    " Life's journey is ...
          not to arrive at the grave safely,
       in a well preserved body,
          but rather to skid in sideways,
       totally burnt out, shouting,
             "HOLY SH*T! WHAT A F*CKING
RIDE!!!"

****
*****

~Thank you Dad. ~
Thank you-
For being a part of my life…
For giving me life.
For helping me become the person I am today
For being a part of me always
For telling me the truth about anything
For teaching me, in many more ways than one,
limitlessly and consistently; how to do things,
how things work, how to fix them(of course),
why people do the

incomprehensible/inconceivable things that they
do;- to understand, learn from, accept,
appreciate, realize, create, imagine, explore,
experience(to the FULLEST), enjoy, determine,
solve, explain, direct, perceive, conquer, invent,
console, charm, support, listen, analyze, focus,
express, motivate, procrastinate, be happy, insist,
operate, generate, and so much more…

But after all,
Isn't that what dads are for?!

Printed in the USA
CPSIA information can be obtained
at www.ICGtesting.com
CBHW070920250924
14863CB00056B/1274